Extremely WEIRD

REPTILES

Text by Sa

John Muir Publications
Santa Fe, New Mexico

Very special thanks to Dale Belcher,
Curator of Herpetology, Rio Grande Zoo

John Muir Publications, P.O. Box 613, Santa Fe, New Mexico 87504

© 1991 by John Muir Publications
All rights reserved. Published 1991
Printed in the United States of America

First edition. Fourth printing January 1993

Library of Congress Cataloging-in-Publication Data
Lovett, Sarah, 1953-
    Extremely weird reptiles / text by Sarah Lovett : [illustrations, Mary
Sundstrom, Sally Blakemore]. — 1st ed.
      p. cm.
    Summary: Describes a variety of reptiles, including the Jackson's chame-
leon, snake-necked turtle of Australia, and eyelash pit viper.
    ISBN 1-56261-036-8
    1. Reptiles—Juvenile literature. [1. Reptiles.] I. Sundstrom, Mary, ill.
II. Blakemore, Sally, ill. III. Title.
  QL644.2.L68 1991
597.9—dc20   91-23161
                                                   CIP
                                                   AC

Extremely Weird Logo Art: Peter Aschwanden
Illustrations: Mary Sundstrom, Sally Blakemore
Design: Sally Blakemore
Typography: Copygraphics, Inc., Santa Fe, New Mexico
Printer: Inland Press

Distributed to the book trade by
W.W. Norton & Co., Inc.
New York, New York

Distributed to the education market by
The Wright Group
19201 120th Avenue N.E.
Bothell, WA 98011-9512

ON THE COVER

Jackson's Chameleon
(Chamaeleo jacksonii)

With cone eyes, scales, bumps, ridges, and horns on its snout, Jackson's chameleon looks like something from another planet. Actually, it's from Africa. In the case of this heady critter, males sport three horns, while females only have one small horn.

   When babies hatch from their shells, they have just tiny bumps on their heads. As they grow, so do the bumps. Two of the male's horns are above the eyes, and the third protrudes from the snout. This headgear is flashy and makes the male very attractive to the female. Horns also serve as weapons when adult males fight each other during the mating season.

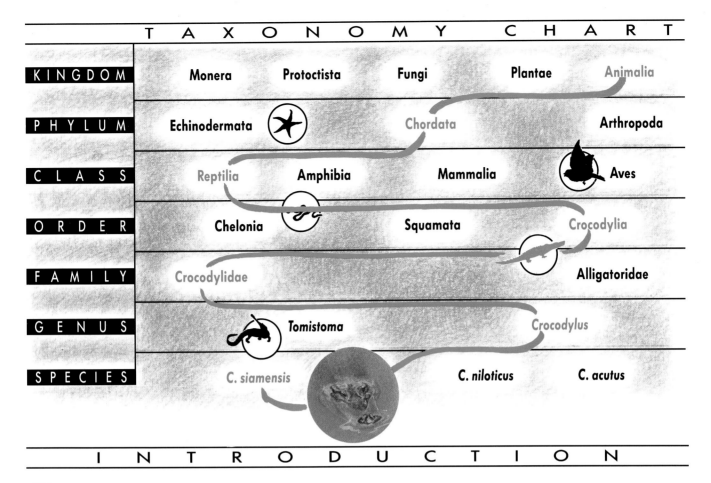

KINGDOM	Monera	Protoctista	Fungi	Plantae	Animalia
PHYLUM	Echinodermata		Chordata		Arthropoda
CLASS	Reptilia	Amphibia	Mammalia		Aves
ORDER	Chelonia		Squamata		Crocodylia
FAMILY	Crocodylidae				Alligatoridae
GENUS	Tomistoma				Crocodylus
SPECIES	C. siamensis		C. niloticus		C. acutus

I N T R O D U C T I O N

R eptiles depend on their outside environment for body heat: they are ectothermic. That's why you might see a snake or a lizard sunbathing on a rock. (Mammals like us, in contrast, have a constant internal body temperature.)

The skin of most reptiles is covered with horny scales or bony plates. Some reptiles have clawed toes, most lay eggs with leathery shells, and their young do not go through a larval stage. (A few reptiles do lay hard-shelled eggs and some give birth to live young.) All reptiles have lungs—even aquatic species—and they breathe air.

Although the Age of Reptiles (which lasted about 120 million years) ended about 70 million years ago, more than 6,500 reptile species exist today. Reptiles live almost everywhere in the world except in the arctic regions.

A few lizards and snakes are poisonous, but most are not dangerous to humans. In fact, reptiles are beneficial because they eat rodents and insects. Many reptile species are endangered by modern dilemmas such as pollution and loss of living space. All reptiles need to be treated with respect by humans.

To keep track of reptiles and the millions of animal and plant species on earth, scientists use a universal system called taxonomy. Taxonomy begins with the five main groups of all living things, the kingdoms, and then divides those into the next group down, phylum, then class, order, family, genus, and finally, species. Members of a *species* look similar, and they can reproduce with each other.

For an example of how taxonomy works, follow the highlighted lines above to see how the Siamese crocodile is classified. In this book, the scientific name of each reptile appears next to the common name. The first word is the genus; the second word is the species.

Turn to the *glossarized index* at the back of this book if you're looking for a specific reptile, for special information (what molting means, for instance), or for the definition of a word you don't understand.

Chuckwalla *(Sauromalus obesus)*

All reptiles are *ecto-thermic* animals, that is, they depend on their outside environment for body heat. Another thing reptiles have in common with each other are backbones, which is why they're known as vertebrates. They also breathe air, lay shelled eggs, and have scales.

More than 250 million years ago, reptiles first crept out of the shallow seas and ventured on land. Of course, the land-lubbing process was gradual. First, reptiles had to develop legs, lungs, scaly skins, and shelled eggs. But the evolutionary effort was worth it; on land, there were plenty of insects to eat and dense forests for shelter. Lizards, turtles, snakes, crocodilians, and the rare tuatara are the five groups of reptiles found on Earth today.

The lizard known as the chuckwalla is blessed with skin as rough, tough, and grainy as sandpaper. Like the desert iguana, the "chuck" needs lots of solar heat to keep its flat, broad body warm and spends much of its day soaking up warmth from rocks and stones in the desert Southwest. When chuckwallas reach old age, and their heaviest weight, they waddle slowly from rock to burrow.

MARY SUNDSTROM

There are about 3,000 species of lizards in the world. They range in size from 1½ inches long to 18 feet! Geckos, skinks, and iguanas are lizards. So is the chameleon.

At the slightest hint of danger, a "chuck" will crawl into a small rock crevice and lock itself in by swelling up its body. Once "anchored," a chuckwalla is almost impossible to move.

There are only two living species of tuataras, or "beak headed" reptiles. Long ago, many different types of these animals flourished on Earth. Today, tuataras are found only on the small islands of New Zealand. Scientists believe tuataras sometimes live as long as 125 years!

Two hundred million years ago, dinosaurs first appeared on earth. Were they reptiles? Although their name comes from two Greek words meaning "terrible lizard," many scientists believe dinosaurs belong to their own class, Dinosauria. In the year 2525, this question will probably still be a question because there are no dinosaurs around to answer it.

SALLY BLAKEMORE

REPTILES

Marine Iguana *(Amblyrhynchus cristatus)*

Marine iguanas live on the Galápagos Islands (off the coast of Ecuador) where they spend much of their day sunning on warm boulders. These animals, who thrive on a diet of seaweed and algae, are the only lizards in the world that feed in salt water. When they swim out to eat, they take great bites of seaweed from ocean rocks using both sides of their jaws—like a dog gnawing on a bone.

Many iguanas have very unusual helmets, or crests, on their heads and a variety of flaps and wrinkles at their throats. Marine iguanas are no exception: they have a mane of rubbery spikes running along their upper backs to the top of their dragonlike heads as well as double or triple chins. When they are trying to frighten off predators or other lizards, they show off their headgear.

Although they're not exactly graceful on land, marine iguanas swim with ease and move through the water quickly. They tuck their legs close to their bodies and move their tails like a large snake.

When naturalist Charles Darwin visited the Galápagos Islands in 1835, he found that both land and marine iguanas had no fear of humans. Since that time, humans have hunted iguanas until very few are left. Now, sadly, these amazing creatures are in danger of extinction.

Many scientists visit the Galápagos Islands because it is such a special world. The animals on these islands evolved in ways that are unique. Sadly, these days, the creatures of the Galápagos are endangered by human activity, just like animals everywhere.

Iguanas come in assorted sizes—4 inches to 7 feet—and they are the most common lizards in Central and South America. But iguanas also live in North America, the West Indies, Madagascar, and the Fiji Islands. In all, there are about 700 species of iguanas in the world.

Photo, facing page, © James P. Rowan

REPTILES

Siamese Crocodile *(Crocodylus siamensis)*

Crocodiles, alligators, and gharials all belong to the reptile group known as crocodilians. These armored and prehistoric-looking creatures are the biggest living reptiles. Some species grow more than 25 feet long! They're also the reptiles most closely related to the ancient dinosaurs.

But don't let all that prehistoric armor fool you—crocodilians are very advanced reptiles when it comes to their hearts. On land, or a nose above water, crocodilians breathe air just like humans. Their heart works like a mammal's four-chambered heart. Used blood is pumped from the body to the heart and finally to the lungs. Refreshed with oxygen in the lungs, the blood makes a return trip—from lungs to heart to body. But when they are submerged in water and holding their breath, crocodilians depend on their reptile hearts. A valve separating the heart chambers opens. Used blood mixes with fresh blood and gets recyled over and over until all the air is used up. Then crocodilians must surface and breathe again—using a four-chambered heart.

Crocodilians are great swimmers and nifty cruisers. Keeping their legs folded close to the body, they whiplash the water with their thick tails. Just like human swimmers, they can kick off the bottom with their hind legs for quick spurts and turns. Crocodiles float in river currents with only their bulging eyes, ears, and nostrils above water. Swimming birds, turtles, and fishes disappear with a snap of the jaws. Even land animals dipping their noses into the water for a drink can be pulled from shore by the powerful grip of crocodile jaws.

Small birds pick parasites off the bodies of one species of crocodilians, the Nile crocodile. They even rush to meet crocs as they emerge from the water. Since they're doing crocodiles a favor, they don't get eaten!

Some species of crocodiles can swim in salt water, and they sometimes travel great ocean distances. Saltwater crocs can grow to lengths of 16 feet, and the record is 32 feet!

Large crocodilians usually spend their nights in water and their days lazing in the sun. To stay cool in midday, they lie with mouths open wide. Like panting dogs, they cool by evaporation.

Mugger crocodiles are believed to be sacred in some parts of India. At a famous crocodile pool in Pakistan, religious pilgrims pay their respects to more than 50 crocodiles who are considered to be priests.

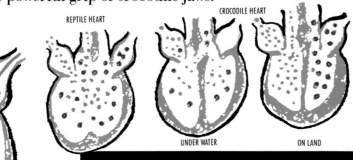

MAMMAL HEART

REPTILE HEART

CROCODILE HEART

UNDER WATER

ON LAND

REPTILES

Here Be Dragons!

Komodo Dragon *(Varanus komodoensis)*

Reaching a length of 10 feet and a weight of 250 pounds, thickly armored and ancient-looking Komodo dragons are one of the the world's largest lizards.

Although Komodo bodies are big, their territory is small. In the wild, they can only be found on Komodo and a few other small islands in Indonesia.

Komodo dragons are flesh eaters. They prey on small wild deer, pigs, and domestic animals. They also work as nature's scavengers, eating the remains of dead animals.

Like all monitor lizards, Komodos have long necks, heavy bodies, and thick tails. They are also equipped with dangerous-looking claws. They use these sharp claws and their equally sharp teeth for tearing their prey into bite-sized chunks. Using a little imagination, Komodos really do look like magnificent dragons.

What's your "habitat"? Since habitat is the place you naturally live, yours might be New York, Detroit, or Amarillo. Komodo dragons have a very limited habitat of a few islands in Indonesia; unlike you, they do not survive anywhere else.

Komodo dragons are big, but another lizard, Salvador's monitor (*Varanus salvadori*), is biggest, reaching lengths of more than 18 feet!

Photo, facing page, courtesy Animals Animals © Miriam Austerman

REPTILES

Spiny Softshell Turtle *(Trionyx spiniferus)*

Turtles are known for their thick armored shells, some of which can support more than 200 times their weight. But softshell turtles are just that; they have to rely on a rubbery shell of skin that has tough cartilage, or gristle, around the edges. Their shells have lost those tough horny plates common to their hard-shelled relatives.

The spiny softshell turtle of North America grows to a length of 18 inches and sports a snorkel-snout for a nose. This "snorkel" acts as a breathing tube for the spiny softshell, who lives completely in water. Spiny softshells can also be found in parts of Asia and Africa. Fossils prove that this turtle also wandered through what is now Europe 65 million years ago.

Although turtles have a reputation for slow going, the spiny softshell is often an active creature. It makes up for its lack of hard-shelled armor by biting and scratching with clawed front feet when it's handled. This softshell is called "spiny" because of the tiny leathery spines covering its back.

Cartoon turtles may be able to leave their shells behind, but real turtles can't! Just like you have a skeleton that stays inside your skin, a turtle's shell protects its soft body for life. The upper shell of a turtle is called the *carapace*. The lower shell protecting the turtle's belly is the *plastron*.

Photo, facing page, courtesy Animals Animals © C. W. Schwartz

REPTILES

Helmeted Lizard (Corytophanes cristatus)

Lizards try a variety of ways to ward off enemies. Some come in colors designed to blend in with the background so they can't be seen. Some leave their tails (or patches of skin) behind to confuse predators while they make their getaway. Others use a special threat display that makes them look big, bigger, biggest! The aim is to look too huge and fierce to tangle with.

For the helmeted lizard, threat posture means the bony "helmet" on the back of its head raises and the skin on its neck swells up. The result is an enormous head. But that's not the end of looking scary. This lizard lifts itself tall on its legs, turns sideways, and its eyes bulge out fiercely. For a final touch, it tips its head down to reveal its helmet.

We humans have our own "threat displays." Have you ever watched a human make a weird face, swell up his or her chest, raise a fist, or swagger down the street? Those are all ways of saying, "Don't mess with me!"

Which came first, the reptile or the egg? Shelled eggs might make you think of chickens and other birds, but really, the first shelled eggs on land were reptilian!

Mexico's two-legged wriggly worm lizard, the ajolote (ah-hoe-LOW-tay), is one of the rarest reptiles in the Western Hemisphere. This lizard uses its two tiny legs (they're only as long as 1/20th of its body length) to burrow into dry, hard ground. When the ajolote is digging into soft ground, its blunt head serves as a bulldozer. It may look like a worm, but it's really a lizard!

REPTILES

Photo, facing page, courtesy Animals Animals

Plumed Basilisk *(Basiliscus plumifrons)*

In the rain forests of Central America lives a very distinguished lizard—the basilisk; it can run on water. For this reason, the basilisk is known by local people as the Jesus Christ lizard. Speedy basilisks have been clocked at speeds of 12 kilometers per hour as they whizz across land or water. Because their toes are widened with skin and they run on their two hind legs at such speeds, they don't have time to sink! They are also moving too fast to be caught by aquatic predators.

Basilisks can start their run across water in three ways. They can begin on land, jump onto water from a branch, or rise to the water's surface. You might call them the triathletes of the lizard world.

But basilisks are not content to skim the waves; they also hang out underwater. They are super swimmers and excellent divers, and they can stay on the bottom of a lake or steam for as long as 30 minutes. That's a nifty way to avoid predators on land.

Mythical monster? No, a basilisk. This little lizard is named for a mythical Greek monster who was half rooster and half snake. Supposedly, the monster's looks could kill by turning you to stone!

The skinny! Lizards (and other reptiles) shed their skin at regular intervals. Large flakes and pieces fall off, and a shiny new skin is already underneath. This process is called molting.

REPTILES

CHAK

Northern Leaf-tailed Gecko (*Phyllurus cornutus*)

With more than 800 different types of geckos spread far and wide over the warm areas of the Earth, these lizards are worldly creatures. Although some species of geckos are silent, their name comes from the "geck-oh" sound that others make.

The northern leaf-tailed gecko has a tail that looks like a leaf. In fact, its head looks like a leaf, too. Its entire body is designed to act as camouflage so it blends in with the background. That way, snakes, birds, cats, and other predators can't see the lizard for the leaf—hopefully!

Another way the leaf-tailed gecko uses its head to protect itself is by using its thick, stumpy tail. Since both ends of this gecko look alike, a hungry predator can hardly tell if the leaf-tailed gecko is coming or going.

Noisy! Some geckos are commonly named for the noises they make. Geckos use their tongues and mouths to "geck," "toke," and "chak." That's why you'll find geckos named "tokay" and "cheekchak."

FOOD?

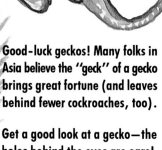

Good-luck geckos! Many folks in Asia believe the "geck" of a gecko brings great fortune (and leaves behind fewer cockroaches, too).

Get a good look at a gecko—the holes behind the eyes are ears!

REPTILES

Tight Squeeze

Green Tree Python *(Chondropython viridis)*

Most people know what snakes look like; they're longish, limbless (without arms and legs), and covered with scales. What about how they sound? At most, you might hear a snake hiss, or rattle, or moan, but snakes are actually mute. Snakes have something else in common; they swallow their prey whole.

Imagine eating a whole cow whole. That would be impossible even if you wanted to try it! But some snakes can swallow a small deer whole. How can a snake get so much food into its mouth at one time? Snake jaws are specially designed for big mouthfuls. The bone that connects the lower jaw to the snake's skull works like a double-jointed hinge: the jaw drops open at the back and the front. Also, the two bones of the lower jaw stretch sideways because its chin muscles are very elastic.

Still hard to believe? Sharp teeth curving toward the snake's throat keep prey in place. Shifting its jaws side to side, bite by bite, the snake then "walks" its mouth over its victim.

Pythons and boas are giants among snakes. They kill their prey by *constriction*. Usually an animal is first caught by the snake's teeth. Then, the snake coils its body around its victim until it suffocates.

Many humans fear snakes, but only four types of constricting snakes are possibly dangerous to humans. Of those, only the South American anaconda is found in the New World. Anacondas have killed humans—but very, very rarely!

All snakes lack eyelids. Instead, their eyes are covered by skin cells. This skinny eyelid is shed when the snake molts, just like the skin on the rest of its body.

Pythons and boas are deaf, but they can "feel" loud noises with their tongues. In fact, a snake's tongue is three sense organs in one—it can touch, smell, and hear.

South American anacondas have been rumored to reach lengths of 40 feet. Reticulated pythons are reliably on record at lengths of 32.5 feet!

Charmed, I'm sure! How do snake charmers train their snakes? They don't. Snakes can't learn tricks, but they can be "handled" by humans. Snake charmers cool their snakes down before a show. A cool snake is slow and passive—and easier to handle. Unfortunately, many human "charmers" do not treat their snakes in a humane way.

REPTILES

Frilled Lizard *(Chlamydosaurus kingi)*

The Australian frilled lizard is famous for its extremely impressive and scaly neck frill. Usually this frill lies like folds of fabric against the lizard's body. But when the frilled lizard feels threatened, it's a different story. If this lizard tightens the muscles connected to its tongue bones, the frill fans out like a great umbrella. The view of a lizard with open mouth and raised frill can be a very threatening sight for would-be predators. That's why this is called a threat posture.

Frilled lizards spend most of their time in trees eating insects. When they do come down to the ground, they run quickly on two hind legs. Frilled lizard tracks look more like bird tracks—only three out of four toes show up.

One relative of the frilled lizard's is the water lizard from the East Indies and New Guinea. These "giants" grow more than 3 feet long.

Another relative, a small lizard called the draco, is known for its flying powers. These animals from Asia and the East Indies have scaly membranes (or "wings") on the sides of their bodies which extend from front to back legs. Dracos glide from tree to tree using their wings to guide them.

REPTILES

Short-horned Chameleon *(Chamaeleo brevicornis)*

If you keep a quick eye on a slow chameleon, you'll notice some special traits. This animal's swiveling eyes move separately and can look at two things at the same time. (Try moving one of your eyes up and the other sideways and see if you can spot a tiny fly!) And all four of a chameleon's feet look as if they've squeezed into scaly mittens. Chameleon tails are handy (and prehensile!)—these lizards use them to grasp tree branches for balance, for climbing, and just for hanging out.

A chameleon's tongue stays bunched up inside its mouth until it's time to catch a grasshopper or other insect. In action, the tongue shoots out lightning quick and insects stick to the clublike padded tip. Finally, both tongue and insect are reeled back in. That may not seem too weird. After all, you can stick out your tongue and then pull it back in. But imagine if your tongue was as long as your body? And imagine if your aim was so sure that you could "lick" an insect on the fly? One thing chameleon tongues *can't* do is stick to damp objects.

Short-horned chameleons from Madagascar are named for the short appendage on their snouts. These critters are especially good at changing colors to match their background, but their change range is only from light yellow to brown. Like many chameleons, they can't turn red or green.

Unlike most lizards, chameleon tails can't be broken off. Chameleons have prehensile tails; they grasp and roll up into perfect spiraling "seashells." Their tails add a special beauty to these little lizards—and also hold onto branches.

Often dull colored, chameleons could be mistaken for tree bark. But true to their names, they do change color. When annoyed, chameleons turn their brightest colors, and so do females about to lay eggs. Chameleons can change shape, too. Flattened, and swaying slowly back and forth, they look like bits of leaves in the wind. These animals are masters of camouflage!

Like all chameleons, the short-horned has cone eyes. Actually, a scale-covered lid surrounds a small opening for the pupil.

Newly hatched or newborn chameleons are on the move and soon! Because they spread out as soon as they can, chameleons don't crowd each other's territory.

DRIVE THRU

BURG

FRI

REPTILES

Eyelash Palm Pit Viper *(Bothriechis schlegelii)*

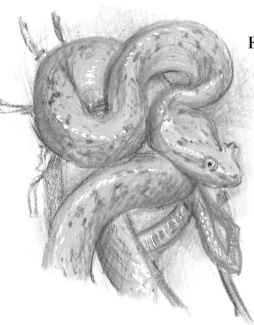

In the forests from Costa Rica to Ecuador, the eyelash pit viper coils in trees, ready to strike. Pit vipers are named for their sixth sense, an organ (or pit) located between each nostril and eye. This organ can sense changes in temperature, which allows the snake to detect body heat given off by prey. With the aid of their sixth sense, pit vipers can strike on target and inject poisonous venom into their victim's body. This is especially handy since the snakes hunt mostly at night, in the dark.

Once a pit viper strikes, its victim usually lives long enough to travel. How does the snake know where to find its wounded prey? Two internal cavities located near the snake's snout connect to its mouth. These are filled with nerve ends (very much like the ones used for smelling) that make it possible for the snake to trail its victim. Often, snakes with this ability also have a separate and very good sense of smell.

The eyelash viper is named for the horny scales above its eyes—a scaly eyelash. Because they are often found in fruit trees, especially bananas, eyelash pit vipers have accidentally traveled to many parts of the world on banana boats.

True vipers are found in Europe, Asia, and Africa.

Water moccasins are pit vipers. They're also the only poisonous water snakes in the United States.

Another pit viper, the North and South American rattlesnake, is part of Native American myth, medicine, religion, and folklore. The world-famous Hopi Indian snake dance lasts nine days. On the last day, priests actually dance with rattlesnakes. When the dance ends, the snakes are released in the four directions, and their job is to carry a positive message to the rain gods. But don't you try dancing with snakes—viper bites can be fatal.

REPTILES

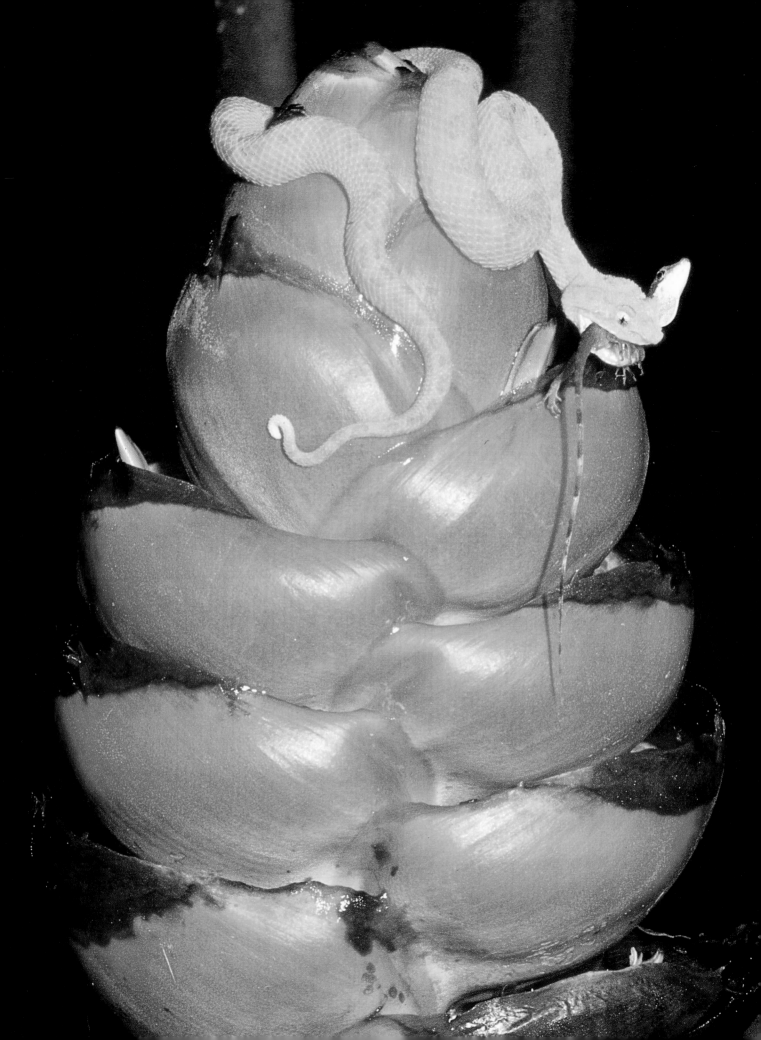

Hide to the Side

Northern Snake-necked Turtle *(Chelodina rugosa)*

With a neck that stretches out like a snake and lots of loose wrinkly skin around its shoulders, the northern snake-necked turtle from Australia won't win any beauty contests. But a turtle's survival success is based on its ability to find food, defend itself, and produce more turtles—not beauty! These swift, nimble, and snappish critters capture small fish with a snakelike forward dart of the neck.

Turtles are the only toothless reptiles. But watch out for your tootsies! Hooked beaks and sharp-edged mouths give turtles plenty of bite.

Good sense! Three of a turtle's senses—sight, smell, and touch—are highly developed.

Of course, the snake-necked turtle has an extra-long neck to protect. This animal, also known as the side-necked turtle, has to bend its neck sideways to hide its head under its shell.

Many humans hunt turtles (and turtle eggs), killing so many that some species have become endangered. But humans have also worshiped turtles for millions of years. Stone Age people left behind small carvings of turtles. Greek legends tell the story of the god Apollo inventing the lyre by tying strings across a sea turtle's shell. African myths speak of a very clever turtle. And for Indians in South America, the turtle is beloved.

Weather or not—male or female? For a number of turtles, the sex of their young seems to be decided by temperature. Warm or cool incubation could mean all male or all female youngsters. Fortunately for both sexes, the weather is always changing!

REPTILES

Photo, facing page. courtesy Animals Animals © Klaus Uhlenhut

Armadillo Lizard *(Cordylus cataphractus)*

The South African armadillo lizard is named for its tough coat of protective scales that look as thick as medieval armor. This slow creature grows to a length of six inches and is especially equipped to defend itself. When threatened, the armadillo lizard puts its tail in its mouth and rolls into a tight ball. This way, predators may get a mouthful of spiny skin, but the lizard's soft belly is protected. The armadillo's layered scales are so thick, they seem as hard as rocks—and not very tasty!

Armadillo lizards are active during the day and spend their time on the ground. Dry ground at that! These animals are found in desert habitats. They can't afford to be particular about how hot it gets or what they eat, and they're not. Over centuries, they've evolved for a perfect fit.

Another armored lizard, the horned toad, lives in North America. When battling with canine or feline predators, this horny creature will squirt jets of blood from its eyes. That could mean a surprise for your cat or dog.

Like horned toads, thorny devils from Australia are ant gourmets. When they find an ant trail, they'll sit and devour the insects for hours.

Photo, facing page, courtesy
Animals Animals © Zig Leszczynski

REPTILES

Galápagos Tortoise (*Geochelone* sp.)

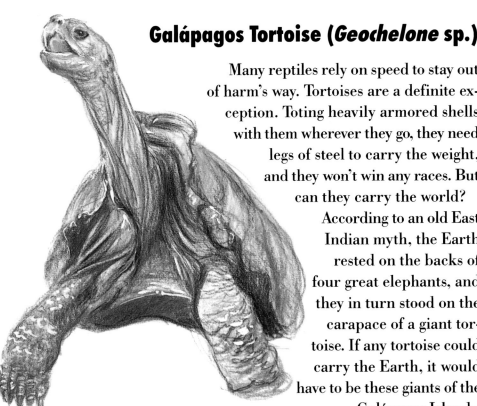

Many reptiles rely on speed to stay out of harm's way. Tortoises are a definite exception. Toting heavily armored shells with them wherever they go, they need legs of steel to carry the weight, and they won't win any races. But can they carry the world?

According to an old East Indian myth, the Earth rested on the backs of four great elephants, and they in turn stood on the carapace of a giant tortoise. If any tortoise could carry the Earth, it would have to be these giants of the Galápagos Islands.

If left alone, the safely armored tortoise can live as long as 150 years.

The tortoise is the most ancient of all reptiles, dating back 250 million years. They haven't changed much since then.

Photo, facing page, courtesy Animals Animals © Breck P. Kent

With their wise eyes, wrinkly faces and necks, scaly bow-legs, and massive shells, Galápagos tortoises look as old as the world. They used to live in great numbers in the Galápagos. Legends say you could walk from an island's end to end on the backs of tortoises without touching the ground. But sailors, whalers, and pirates who stopped at the islands slaughtered the tortoises for fresh meat. And later settlers brought rats, dogs, cats, and wild pigs that also killed them.

Although some kinds of Galápagos tortoises are extinct, a number still survive.

REPTILES

Shingleback Skink (*Trachydosaurus rugosus*)

Skinks come in about 800 species, and they live in the warmer areas of the earth. Although there are many varieties, most skinks are very similar in color, shape, and habit.

The shingleback skink—a.k.a. the pine cone, stump-tail, bobtail, or double-headed lizard—is a dark brown, scaly critter that does have a tail that is short, stumpy, and looks much like its head. Two heads are better than one when a predator is trying to figure out which way a skink will try to run. Also, the fat stored in the skink's tail comes in very handy when food is scarce.

When offered the chance, shinglebacks will eat snails, slugs, ants, small animals, and carcasses—almost anything! They even eat small stones to help digest their food. They are very clean reptiles to have around.

When threatened, shinglebacks have a surprise for their enemies. They hiss and open their mouths to show off their gray blue tongues.

Shinglebacks don't lay eggs. Instead, their babies (usually there are two or three) are born live.

Shinglebacks are called that because the heavy, bony scales on their backs lay over each other just like the shingles on your roof.

REPTILES

American Alligator (*Alligator mississippiensis*)

Less than 20 years ago, American alligators had almost disappeared from planet Earth because humans were killing them for their hides, for sport, and to make room for more humans. Now, because of strong laws against poaching and because these animals are hearty, American alligators have returned to many parts of Florida, Louisiana, and nearby states. These reptiles seem to adapt easily to human neighbors.

American alligators have been known to grow more than 19 feet long. But the average size is more like 6 to 12 feet.

Female American alligators are good mothers. They build nests—big enough for several humans to fit inside—of mud and grass and stay close by for several months while eggs incubate. There may be 20 to 70 hard-shelled eggs per nest. The mother grunts to her eggs gently, and when the babies are finally ready to hatch, they chirrup back. This way, the female knows it's time to help with the hatching.

Parents of some crocodilians help open eggs and carry babies to water for a bath. Babies stay close to their parents for several years. They are often seen hitching a crocodile-back ride on their parents.

Although they do spend time out of water, crocodilians are clumsier with all four feet on dry land.

American alligator eggs are about as big as a goose egg.

Alligators have not changed much during the 200 million years they've existed on Earth.

Some humans swim with plugs in their ears and noses to keep from getting waterlogged. Crocodilians don't need extra equipment. Valves in their ears and nostrils shut out water below the water line.

GRUNT

CHIRRUP

REPTILES

South American Matamata Turtle *(Chelus fimbriatus)*

With its flat head, flexible snorkle, and long neck with shaggy flaps of skin, the matamata turtle is probably one of the weirdest-looking of all reptiles. Its body resembles a pile of muck and leaves. But weird looks are no hardship for the matamata —instead, it's great camouflage. To small fish and aquatic animals, this turtle's fringed and lumpy body must seem like something good to nibble on. When fish swim too close, watch out! The matamata's head shoots out, its rubbery jaws and throat open wide, and water—containing any nearby food—is sucked inside like dust into a vacuum cleaner.

The matamata is a very quiet turtle. In fact, you'd hardly know it's around. It is most active at twilight and after dark. Like crocodiles, the back of the matamata's eyes have a crystalline lining that reflects light. It gives these turtle eyes an eerie gleam.

The alligator snapper is a turtle with a twist. In muddy water, it looks like part of the river or lake bottom. There it waits, jaws open. If you could see inside its mouth, you'd see a built-in "worm." This bait is actually part of the turtle's mouth. When fish swim near, alligator snappers wiggle their "worms" enticingly, and then they strike, sure and lightning fast. Snap!

REPTILES

Photo, facing page, courtesy Animals Animals © Zig Leszczynski

Land Iguana *(Conolophus subcristatus)*

Most iguanas eat insects, spiders, and other small animals, but a few of the larger species are vegetarians. Found only on the Galápagos Islands, stocky, round-tailed land iguanas eat mouthfuls of cactus spines without feeling the prick or stick. In fact, they even look a bit like a cactus plant with their tough skins and rubbery spikes. These animals roam the islands like venerable dragons, but there aren't as many land iguanas as there used to be.

On his visit in 1835, naturalist Charles Darwin reported there were so many iguanas, there was hardly room to pitch a tent. Now, they have completely disappeared on some islands because of human predators.

Long ago, iguanas probably arrived on the Pacific Islands (from the continents) via floating logs and objects sailing on the ocean's currents.

So many animals are endangered —what can you do to help? You can join an environmental group and you can help support your local zoo. Many zoos have special programs for endangered animals. Another way to help endangered animals is by limiting world population growth of humans. As the planet becomes more and more crowded with people, there is less and less room for other living species.

40

REPTILES

Photo, facing page, courtesy Animals Animals © Patti Murray

Emerald Tree Monitor *(Varanus prasinus)*

Tropical monitor lizards come in a variety of sizes—from 8 inches to 18 feet long! Depending upon the species, habits vary, also. Some monitors stay on the ground, avoiding water and trees almost always, while others swim easily, climb tall trees, and burrow underground with ease. All monitor lizards are diurnal, which means they are active during the day.

A monitor lizard's diet may include fish, frogs, crabs, birds, eggs, small mammals, even larger mammals and decaying meat. Of course, an 8-inch lizard won't eat a pig, but a 10-foot Komodo dragon will!

Emerald tree monitors live in the trees of the forests of New Guinea where they grasp branches with their flexible, prehensile tails.

Species of monitor lizards come in various sizes—generally large. Because of their size, they don't worry about as many predators as other lizards. Monitor lizards must be on the lookout for crocodiles, birds of prey, and large meat-eating mammals. Of course, their most dangerous enemies are humans!

A favorite snack for emerald tree monitors are katydids.

On the run from hungry predators, a lizard may leave its tail behind to attract attention—while the rest of the lizard gets away. Lizards have this ability to ''de-tail'' because of special bones in their backbone. New tails grow back soon—sometimes as many as 2 or 3 at once!

...to, facing page, courtesy Animals Animals

Feet Feats!

Hasselquist's Gecko *(Ptyodactylus hasselquistii)*

Some geckos are clingy climbers with feet capable of sticky feats! The bottom of a gecko's toes are designed with clinging pads. A closer look shows these pads are covered with microscopic hairs. These teensy hairs have blunt ends that press against small surface areas and give most geckos "sticky power." On the move, geckos can climb trees, scale walls, and even cruise on the ceiling with the greatest of ease.

Hasselquist's gecko (a.k.a. "house gecko") has a big head and bulging eyes. This gecko's foot pads are shaped like fans and give it special adhesive powers. Hasselquist's gecko also sports claws at the ends of its toes.

During mating season, male and female pairs of these geckos, who live in Algeria, Central Sahara, Iraq, and Iran, stake out their territory and defend it. Hasselquist's geckos are known to live as long as 10 years.

Besides climbing, some geckos also fly. At least, they glide. With wide flaps of skin on each side of its body and webbed feet, Asiatic forest geckos can glide from tree to tree.

All geckos (except a few species in New Zealand) lay eggs.

Some people believe that geckos are poisonous and dangerous to humans. Wrong! Although a gecko bite might hurt, it won't do any permanent damage.

REPTILES

This glossarized index will help you find specific reptile information. It will also help you understand the meaning of some of the words used in this book.

BOOKS FOR YOUNG READERS AGES 8 AND UP

from John Muir Publications

X-ray Vision Series

Each title in the series is 8½" x 11", 48 pages, $9.95, paperback, with four-color photographs and illustrations and written by Ron Schultz.

Looking Inside the Brain
Looking Inside Cartoon Animation
Looking Inside Sports Aerodynamics
Looking Inside Sunken Treasure
Looking Inside Telescopes and the
  Night Sky

Masters of Motion Series

Each title in the series is 10¼" x 9", 48 pages, $9.95, paperback, with four-color photographs and illustrations.

How to Drive an Indy Race Car
  David Rubel
How to Fly a 747
  Tim Paulson
How to Fly the Space Shuttle
  Russell Shorto

The "Extremely Weird" Series

All of the titles are written by Sarah Lovett, 8½" x 11", 48 pages, and $9.95 paperbacks.

Extremely Weird Bats
Extremely Weird Birds
Extremely Weird Endangered Species
Extremely Weird Fishes
Extremely Weird Frogs
Extremely Weird Insects
Extremely Weird Primates
Extremely Weird Reptiles
Extremely Weird Sea Creatures
Extremely Weird Spiders

Other Titles of Interest

Habitats
Where the Wild Things Live
Randi Hacker and Jackie Kaufman
8½" x 11", 48 pages, color illustrations,
$9.95 paper

The Indian Way
*Learning to Communicate with
Mother Earth*
Gary McLain
Painting by Gary McLain
Illustrations by Michael Taylor
7" x 9", 114 pages, two-color illustrations,
$9.95, paper

**Kids Explore America's African-American
Heritage**
Westridge Young Writers Workshop
7" x 9", 112 pages, illustrations and
photographs, $8.95, paper

Kids Explore America's Hispanic Heritage
Westridge Young Writers Workshop
7" x 9", 112 pages, illustrations and
photographs, $7.95, paper

Rads, Ergs, and Cheeseburgers
*The Kids' Guide to Energy and the
Environment*
Bill Yanda
Illustrated by Michael Taylor
7" x 9", 108 pages, two-color illustrations,
$13.95, paper

The Kids' Environment Book
What's Awry and Why
Anne Pedersen
Illustrated by Sally Blakemore
7" x 9", 192 pages, two-color illustrations,
$13.95, paper

The Quill Hedgehog Adventure Series

Green fiction for young readers. Each title is written by John Waddington-Feather and illustrated by Doreen Edmond.

Quill's Adventures in the Great Beyond
BOOK ONE
5½" x 8½", 96 pages, $5.95, paper

Quill's Adventures in Wasteland
BOOK TWO
5½" x 8½", 132 pages, $5.95, paper

Quill's Adventures in Grozzieland
BOOK THREE
5½" x 8½", 132 pages, $5.95, paper

The Kidding Around Travel Guides

All of the titles listed below are 64 pages and $9.95 except for *Kidding Around the National Parks* and *Kidding Around Spain*, which are 108 pages and $12.95.

"A combination of practical information, vital statistics, and historical asides."
—New York Times

Kidding Around Atlanta
Kidding Around Boston, 2nd ed.
Kidding Around Chicago, 2nd ed.
Kidding Around the Hawaiian Islands,
Kidding Around London
Kidding Around Los Angeles
Kidding Around the National Parks
  of the Southwest
Kidding Around New York City, 2nd ed.
Kidding Around Paris
Kidding Around Philadelphia
Kidding Around San Diego
Kidding Around San Francisco
Kidding Around Santa Fe
Kidding Around Seattle
Kidding Around Spain
Kidding Around Washington, D.C., 2nd ed.